This Journal Belongs To:

Made in the USA
Monee, IL
18 January 2022

89280243R00056